Original title:
Love in a Clay Pot

Copyright © 2025 Creative Arts Management OÜ
All rights reserved.

Author: Natalia Harrington
ISBN HARDBACK: 978-1-80581-739-0
ISBN PAPERBACK: 978-1-80581-266-1
ISBN EBOOK: 978-1-80581-739-0

Molding Moments into Memories

In the garden of clay, we play and spin,
Mixing laughter with a splash of grin.
With every squish and squabble, we make our mark,
As pots of humor light up the dark.

Fingers coated with mud, we dance around,
Crafting odd shapes, joy knows no bound.
Watch that wonky vase wobble and sway,
As we charm the silly with every play.

Whirl of Emotion on the Wheel

Round and round, on the wheel we go,
A dizzying ride, don't put on a show!
With each spin, our giggles collide,
As the clay takes shape and so does our pride.

You dip, I dive, in this happy mess,
Who knew mud would spark such deep happiness?
A pot might wobble, but we won't fret,
For unfinished dreams are our best duet.

The Art of Holding Together

In the kiln of chaos, we find our way,
Holding hands while we smoosh and play.
Our masterpieces may crack, but we still shine,
For every little blunder is a sign divine.

With a pinch of humor, we mend each fold,
No two pots alike, but each tale is bold.
Creating art that's quirky and bright,
In our crafty chaos, everything feels right.

Fragile Forms of Lasting Passion

These pots may wobble, but oh, what a sight,
With glazes that sparkle and colors so bright.
We sculpt our dreams like playful kids,
Turning mishaps into treasures, that's how love lives.

Each crack tells a story, of trials and cheer,
In the world of clay, there's nothing to fear.
For when we get messy, that's when we laugh,
Making memories stronger with every mishap.

Pottery of the Soul

In a workshop full of clay,
Where hearts mix up their sway,
A vase spoke up with a giggle,
"I'm not just a pot, I'm a wiggle!"

Crafting art with such charm,
Avoiding every alarm,
"Watch out for the kiln's warm kiss,"
"Or I might turn into a miss!"

Holding Dreams in Terra Cotta

With dreams tossed in a bowl,
And petals filling a role,
A cheeky jug starts to dance,
"Join me in this silly prance!"

Each flower's a hopeful fling,
In the sunlight, they all sing,
"Watch your petals, don't let them slip,"
"Or off they'll go on a clay trip!"

The Warmth Beneath the Surface

Underneath a pot's great rim,
Lies warmth that makes us grin,
A little worm peeks right through,
"Excuse me, did someone say stew?"

The clay giggles, softly bright,
As it warms up the cool night,
"Let's create a feast so grand,"
"A salad served by little hand!"

Roots Intertwined in Ceramics

In a garden of strange pots,
Where tangled roots make knots,
A cactus borrows a line,
"Hey, don't let my thorns decline!"

And with a wink from each bloom,
They dispel all the gloom,
"Together we'll grow and sway,"
"Making pottery our play!"

Fired with Intent

In a studio, we play with mud,
Spinning dreams with every thud.
You giggle while I mold and shape,
A pot of joy, a silly cape.

Laughter erupts, what a goof!
A wobbly vase, it's just aloof.
My masterpiece, a lopsided thrill,
But it sure makes you laugh, oh what a skill!

Hand in Hand through Shaping

Two hands together, let's craft a mess,
You splash me with clay, I must confess.
With giggles and grins, we spin the wheel,
Making pottery, oh what a deal!

I shape a bowl, you toss it aside,
You say it's art, I say it's my pride.
Sculpting our way through chaos with glee,
In this clay dance, just you and me.

Earthy Rhythms of Belonging

We stomp on the ground, play like a fool,
As mud flies around, we both break the rule.
Our feet in the clay, it's a slippery scene,
Creating our chaos, like nothing you've seen.

You sing out a tune, while I slip and trip,
A clay-covered dream, we savor each slip.
Like pottery shapes in playful embrace,
Our laughter forms bonds that none can erase.

The Weight of Belonging

With every pot made, there's charm in the cracks,
You trip over clay while I dodge the flaks.
Our love's like the kiln—fired and bright,
But just watch your step, oh what a sight!

In the warmth of our chaos, we find our way,
With mugs full of laughter to bright up the day.
Together we stand in this clay-dusted whirl,
Two quirky artists, my partner, my girl!

Whispering Vows in Stone

In a garden of pebbles, we make our stand,
Laughter rolls like marbles, so close at hand.
Fingers clay-muddied, our promises sway,
Sculpting odd hearts, in a playful array.

With giggles and winks, we twist and we mold,
Each silly mishap, a story retold.
As we chip and we crack, we both start to see,
Two quirky figures, in perfect harmony.

Waiting to be Fired

Two lumps of soft clay, we sit side by side,
Cracking jokes as we wait, never one for pride.
Our plans are all wobbly, but hey, that's okay,
We'll warm up our hearts in the most comical way.

Like pots in the kiln, we're both feeling tense,
Hoping our jokes lead to some fun recompense.
In the heat of the moment, let's chuckle and cheer,
For the quirks that we cherish are what we revere.

Sacred Spaces in Building Blocks

With bricks stacked so whimsically high,
We build up our dreams, oh me, oh my!
Each block has a story, a giggle, a sigh,
Creating a fortress, where laughter can fly.

In this cobbled-up chaos, we wiggle and dance,
Every bump in the woodwork gives love a chance.
Sacred, yet silly, in corners we play,
Our hearts are the foundation, come what may.

Tactile Affections

With fingers so sticky, we tackle our fate,
Molding our moments, it's never too late.
Our touches are goofy, yet sweet as can be,
In this quirky adventure, it's just you and me.

Like clay on the wheel, we spin with delight,
Laughter's the glaze that makes everything right.
Our lives craft a canvas, so vibrant, so free,
In this silly embrace, we just let it be.

Echoes of Affection

In a garden of laughter, we play,
With pots that giggle, come what may.
They wobble and dance, so absurdly round,
Whispers of joy are all around.

A flower tried flirting, fell in a ditch,
Its sprightly petals give me a hitch.
The soil grins wide, it's all in good fun,
As we pot our dreams beneath the sun.

Molded Memories

A pot made of clay, how silly it seems,
Yet holds all the wonders of our wild dreams.
We shape silly hearts with every new twist,
In each little crack, there's a moment missed.

Jokes in the garden, with weeds that they tease,
"Just pot me up, if you please!"
We giggle as petals scatter and soar,
In memories shaped from the clay we adore.

Heartstrings in Porcelain

A cup half-full serves tea and old jokes,
As we sip laughter, turn up the hoaxes.
The saucer joins in, oh what a sight,
Chasing the crumbs of a sweet, silly bite.

Spinning our stories on whimsical wheels,
Each slip and trip, oh how one feels!
With porcelain hearts, we chime in delight,
Crafting our tales under pale moonlight.

Affection's Clay Craft

With hands in the clay, we mold and we twist,
A bumpy bouquet, just look at this fist!
Each scoop of the earth, our giggles ignite,
Creating a mess that feels just right.

Baking our laughter, firing our dreams,
In sculpts of the night, where nothing redeems.
A chuckle erupts from the pot's little grin,
In mud-coated hearts, that's where we begin.

Sculpted Dreams Beneath the Moon

In a garden of mismatched shoes,
We dance like pots with cracks and grooves.
Our laughter mingles with the breeze,
As we fashion hearts with clumsy ease.

Under the starlit, glazed domain,
We toss our worries, free from strain.
Though mud and grit may paint our face,
Each slip just adds to our embrace.

Claybound Secrets of the Heart

With silly grins, we start to mold,
A sculpted tale, both shy and bold.
Whispers echo through the clay,
Of antics that we'll joke about today.

Each fumbled piece, a quirky charm,
In our playful dance, there's no alarm.
With every blob and gooey mess,
We find sweet joy in pure excess.

A Radiant Touch in Porcelain

Oh, the tea cups tremble with our cheer,
As we share secrets, sip by sip, my dear.
Fingers sticky, laughter spills,
In porcelain dreams, our spirit thrills.

With every brush stroke, we mistake,
A smear of joy, a pop of quirk-like cake.
We'll paint the world in shades so bright,
Even if we start a friendly fight!

The Artwork of Us

We sculpt our dreams with humor's grace,
Creating joy in every space.
Like quirky pots with wiggly lines,
We sparkle bright, even when we're pine.

From mismatched glazes to odd designs,
Every flub's a tale that brightly shines.
In the gallery of mishaps, we reside,
Giggles and snorts forever our guide.

Whispers of Earthen Embrace

In a corner garden, tucked away,
Two clay souls giggle in the sun's play.
They spill their secrets, cheeky and bold,
While the daisies blush as stories unfold.

One pot says, "I've got a crack, you see!"
The other replies, "We'll grow wild and free!"
Together they dream of a world so bright,
With mossy hats and stars in the night.

Tender Heartbeats in Terra Cotta

A terra cotta heart, so round and sweet,
Twirling with joy at the rhythm of feet.
Each thump and bump makes the gardener smile,
As they wiggle and dance, quite out of style.

Caught in the rain, they laughed at the storm,
As puddles splashed, they took on new form.
Their laughter echoed in the moist air,
With every giggle, they lightened the stare.

The Dance of Hand-formed Affection

Two pots on a shelf, well-crafted and neat,
Go twirling and spinning to a whimsical beat.
With every sway, they topple and tip,
In their joy, they forget their tight grip.

Molded with care, yet filled with delight,
They make quite the scene, a comical sight.
With each little tumble, they cackle and roll,
In the garden of giggles, they find their soul.

Vessels of Passion Beneath the Stars

Under the twilight, two vases conspire,
With hopes and dreams, they spark a desire.
"Hey, I'm more handsome!" one boasts with flair,
"Just fill me with dirt, and you've made a pair!"

Stars twinkle down, give a wink or two,
As petals and weeds join this funny crew.
With laughter they flourish, unique in their way,
Creating a banquet for the critters to play.

Textured Moments

In a world of wild clay spins,
We shape our dreams with silly grins.
Each bump a chuckle, each swirl a tease,
Molding laughter like a warm gentle breeze.

With every pinch, I make a face,
A masterpiece born from a silly place.
You drop the dough, I laugh so loud,
Together we dance, feeling quite proud.

Sculpting hearts with a twist and a turn,
In this playful art, we passionately yearn.
Crafted moments in each little crack,
With laughter and clay, we never look back.

Pottery's Silent Serenade

On the wheel we spin like dizzy mops,
As laughter fills in all the empty gaps.
The clay sings softly, a humorous tune,
While we both bumble, blessed by the moon.

With rolling pins, we duel like knights,
In our kitchen arena, we face the heights.
A doughy disaster, but oh what a show,
We crack up together, just watch how we glow.

Each slip of the hand brings a chuckle anew,
Our masterpiece waits, but first, let's brew!
With joy and some mess, we mold our own charms,
In the soft glow of our whimsical farms.

Adorned by Life

With glitter and glaze, we paint with delight,
In this banquet of clay, everything's bright.
You glue on a flower, I stick on a cactus,
All the weird shapes? Well, we just can't pass this!

Our pots wear their quirks like a badge of pride,
Wobbly edges, no place to hide.
We giggle as we sculpt, it's totally neat,
With every odd angle, our vision's complete.

In the chaos of craft, we find such glee,
Adorned by life, just you and me.
A riot of colors that brighten the day,
Our funny little kingdom, come what may.

A Meeting of Minds

Two artists collide in a whirl of clay,
Mixing our thoughts in a playful ballet.
With puns and a wink, we spin with flair,
Creating our stories, who needs a fair?

A lump of joy, a sprinkle of fate,
Forming our dreams at this muddy gate.
With every mistake, we burst into cheer,
A funny endeavor, no worries, my dear.

The wheel keeps turning, laughter's our guide,
In this school of clay, we take it in stride.
Each quirky pot, a tale we ignite,
A meeting of minds that feels just right!

The Art of Together

Two hands in the mud, what a sight,
Laughter erupts, oh what delight!
Molding our dreams, some take a twist,
Each quirky curve, none can resist.

With every splash, splatters and play,
We dance in the chaos, hip-hip-hooray!
A masterpiece born of giggles and mess,
A crafted treasure, nothing less.

Embracing Imperfection

A crack on the pot, what a tale to tell,
Each flaw reveals a charm—goodbye, wishing well!
We find silver linings in uneven seams,
Our art is perfect, or so it seems.

The glaze runs wild, what a funky hue,
Mixing odd colors, a vibrant view!
From mismatched patterns comes pure joy,
A quirky treasure, oh yes, oh boy!

Kiln-Fired Promises

In the oven of trust, we're baking away,
Hot air rises, our dreams in full sway!
With every puff, we hold our breath tight,
Will it burst to pieces or come out just right?

A promise sealed in a fiery embrace,
We laugh as we watch it, what a race!
Every crack and chip, a story to share,
Tender and tough, life's a comedy fair.

Duality in the Drying

One pot is dry, the other still wet,
A face-off of patience, a funny duet!
We giggle and shuffle, what a strange show,
One's eager to shine, the other moves slow.

With timings askew, we dance on a line,
Wishing for harmony, feeling divine!
In the end, we learn it's quite alright,
In the world of ceramics, there's always delight.

Luminous Hues of Belonging

In a kitchen nook, pots abound,
Laughter echoes, a joyous sound.
With each clatter, we create a stir,
Mixing ingredients with a cheeky slur.

Mismatched plates, but hearts align,
Whipped cream fights for a share of wine.
In our chaos, sweet moments bloom,
Clumsy dances in the small room.

Finding joy in spilled tomato stew,
A splash of basil, a dance for two.
Here's to the mess, our quirky art,
Crafted together, we never part.

Fragmented Love

Cracks in the surface, yet we shine,
Peanut butter and jelly, so divine.
Like jigsaw pieces, we fit just right,
Even when we turn a food fight.

Chipped edges hold memories dear,
Each awkward hug draws us near.
Sipping tea from a cracked old cup,
In the end, it's more than enough.

A sprinkle of salt on banana bread,
Uneven dancing, yet we're fed.
Finding laughter where chaos lays,
In our kitchen, joy ablaze.

Whole Again

When the mug breaks, we just smile,
Jokes about splinters go for miles.
Each piece tells a story anew,
Wobbly cupcakes we try to chew.

There's magic in our scrapes and scars,
Burnt toast leads to sweet repars.
With every spill, a giggle erupts,
In our silly world, love interrupts.

A recipe gone wrong merely adds,
To our tales of silly fads.
Dough on the ceiling, laughter rings,
In this chaos, we find new flings.

The Garden of Heart's Clay

Planting seeds with a wink and a grin,
Watering each sprout, where to begin?
Petunias giggle beneath the sun,
As we chase squirrels just for fun.

Tangled weeds, our playful fight,
Dancing through shadows, chasing light.
With muddy hands and laughter loud,
We toss our worries in the crowd.

Sunflowers nod as if they know,
The secrets of love in our show.
Snapdragons snap, a funny affair,
In our garden, joy fills the air.

Eternal Embrace in Terra

In the pot's embrace, we find our way,
Cooking up dreams in a quirky display.
Sauce spilled here, laughter there,
In our banquet, we've little care.

Airy dough flies, a flour fight,
Who knew baking could feel so right?
Caffeinated chatter with quirky puns,
Under the warmth of kitchen suns.

Root vegetables dance, they wiggle and roll,
In our kitchen, we feel so whole.
With each bite, bizarre tales unfold,
A recipe rich with laughter and gold.

Tender Embrace of Earth

In a garden bed with a cheeky grin,
Two hearts grow wild, where the roots begin.
They dance in the breeze, doing silly twirls,
Whispering secrets like playful squirrels.

With muddy hands and a wink so sly,
They sculpt a future beneath the sky.
A pot of laughter, a dash of fun,
Building their dreams with each rising sun.

Whispers of the Hearth

By the firelight, they joke and tease,
Building up warmth with delicious ease.
A cauldron of giggles, simmering slow,
Bubbling over with feelings that glow.

They toss in some spice with a pinch of cheer,
Stirring up moments that bring them near.
With every chuckle, their hearts intertwine,
Creating a recipe too good to resign.

Clay-Kissed Hearts

Two quirky shapes in a potter's hands,
Joking and laughing, making grand plans.
With a splash of clay and a roll of dough,
Their laughter erupts like a majestic show.

As they spin on the wheel, they giggle and squeak,
Molding together, week after week.
With a glaze of glee, they shine and sway,
Crafting their journey in a playful way.

Cherished Impressions

In a bustling studio, they mix and mold,
Creating memories, a sight to behold.
With a wink and a nudge, they shape the clay,
Masterpieces born in a whimsical way.

Each pot has stories that flourish and grow,
Funky designs with a comedic flow.
With hands sticky sweet and hearts so bright,
They craft their joy in the morning light.

Marbled Hearts

In a kitchen filled with flour,
Two hearts mix like dough, oh what power.
Rolling pins clash, laughter spills,
Baking that love, oh what thrills!

With frosting fights and silly grins,
Love is sweet with all our sins.
Cakes rise high, but we trip low,
Flour on noses, what a show!

Traces of My Heart

A cookie trail leads to my heart,
Each bite we take, a sugary start.
Crumbs on your shirt, you look so sweet,
With each silly mishap, my heart skips a beat.

Frosting on lips, it's quite the sight,
You're a messy lover, but it feels so right.
Ovens blast heat, but we're cooler still,
In this fun chaos, you fit the bill!

Clay and Warmth

With fingers dipped in muddy clay,
We sculpt our dreams in a playful way.
A pot so lopsided, yet full of glee,
Each twist and turn, I'm glad it's we!

When it cracks, it's a joke we share,
Repairing it quick while pulling your hair.
Warmth in our hearts, despite the mess,
Like clay, we mold, not seek to impress!

Mosaic of Affection

With tiles and glue, we craft our fate,
A funky masterpiece, oh, isn't it great?
Each piece a moment, a goofy time,
Stuck together, a love in its prime.

Jigsaw puzzles gone awry,
Your crooked smile, my favorite tie.
In this funny chaos, we fit so right,
A mosaic of joy, oh what a sight!

Spaces Filled with Touch

In a pot so round and wide,
We planted dreams side by side,
Molded hopes with gentle hands,
Danced together, like good bands.

Marbles rolling, laughter spills,
Silly faces, heartbeats thrill,
Serve the soup of joy with flair,
Watch it slosh, oh what a scare!

Pasta curls and sauce goes splat,
In our vessel, we both sat,
Planting beans and jokes galore,
With each stitch, what's yet in store?

Coffee drips, a playful fight,
Our clay pot's become a light,
From spoon to heart, the mix is grand,
In this chaos, we just stand.

Eternal Crafted Connection

In the kiln of time we meet,
Shape our dreams with playful beat,
There's a crack, a tiny smile,
Glazed in joy, let's stay awhile.

Mold me silly, twist my fate,
With each turn, I feel more great,
Let's fire up our antics bright,
With every laugh, we take flight.

Sculpting moments, nerdy clay,
Smooth it over, come what may,
Cheeky puns, we bond and cling,
As chimneys puff, let's make them sing!

In our pot where magic's shared,
Crafting giggles, none impaired,
Let's embrace our quirky path,
With every cringe, I do the math.

The Balance of Creation

In the artful dance of clay,
We shape our quirks, come what may,
Balancing the laughs and sighs,
Like a pot that never dries.

Spinning round on this wild wheel,
Heavy grins share every meal,
Flipping jokes with every turn,
In our hearts, the candles burn.

A splash of paint, a dash of fun,
Mixing bright until we're done,
Tip the pot and watch it flow,
Laughter's soup, in tide we row.

Cracks appearing? No big deal!
We'll just patch it with a seal,
In our crafty, cozy space,
We'll create our unique place.

A Symphony in Clay

In our little pot of dreams,
We compose with silly beams,
From fingertips, the rhythm flows,
As the potter's wheel just goes.

Tunes of clay, let's sing along,
Bakes our hearts, a brazen song,
Playful beats in every crack,
With a smile, we won't hold back.

With the mallet, a hearty thump,
Joy ignites, we twirl and jump,
Each lyric laughs, each verse a hug,
In our vessel, oh so snug!

From the oven, our harmony,
Made in smiles, it's pure folly,
This symphony, no need for scripts,
In a pot, our hearts eclipse.

Poetry in Pottery

A jug that tilts, a cup that slips,
Our dance involves some clumsy trips.
With mugs and pots, we play a game,
Each drip and drop, we stake our claim.

Your laughter rings in earthenware,
While I pretend that I don't care.
But with each crash and every crack,
My heart does somersaults, no lack.

We sculpt our dreams with playful hands,
In a world made of soft, muddy sands.
Your eyes shine bright; I can't resist,
In the kiln's warm hug, we coexist.

So here's to pots and all they hold,
Our jokes shared in the fiery mold.
Each piece we throw, a story spun,
In this hilarious game, we've already won.

Timeless Earthbound Affection

In the garden of clay where we dig,
You stuck your foot in, thinking it's big.
With floury hands, we start to mold,
A treasure or mess? The tale's yet told.

You pinch a rim, I reshape a base,
Our masterwork, a lopsided vase.
But oh, its charm in all its flaws,
With each ugly crack, our laughter roars.

The wheel spins round, a dizzying fate,
We toss our dreams—let's plan a date!
Tonight, we feast from bowls we made,
Though chips and cracks will not evade.

Together we stand, hands covered in clay,
Creating sweet chaos in our own way.
In the land of pottery, we're never dismayed,
For even if bent, our hearts will cascade.

Secrets in the Kiln

What's baking inside? A pot of good cheer,
Piling up stories, and maybe some beer!
With a swirl of colors, we find our groove,
Each laugh is a echo, each moment a move.

You whisper to mugs while they spin and sway,
"Will we ever host dinner?" I chuckle and say,
"Only if they come with, a side of potato,
And everyone brings their own funny dado!"

The kiln holds secrets, hot as the sun,
With mishaps unfurling, oh so much fun.
From funky vases to cups cracked with care,
Our creations are treasures, mood in the air.

So when we unveil our art full of glee,
We toast to the madness, you, and me.
For every odd piece is a tale well spun,
In this chaotic dance, we have already won.

The Space Between Us

Two chairs side by side, both made of clay,
Perhaps that's enough to brighten our day.
You say, "Move closer," I feign to ignore,
"Not till this ashtray can hold even more!"

Wobbly pots dance in a circular game,
Each spin brings laughter; it's never the same.
You throw a ball—oh, watch it unfold,
It lands in the kiln, where surprises are gold!

An awkward silence, as glazes take flight,
We craft our admissions late into the night.
Though a pot may break, or the wheel may wobble,
Our banter and smiles will always hobble.

So here we are, in this muddy expanse,
Firing off puns, as we giggle and dance.
The space that divides us? A pot full of cheer,
In this world of clay, there's nothing to fear.

In the Hands of Creation

With hands of mud and pots that spin,
A masterpiece begins to grin.
Short bottom, a wide top douse,
Can this hold my heart, or just a mouse?

Laughter echoes in the kiln's warm breath,
Fired up, will it survive, or meet its death?
A cup for tea, or a vase for fools,
Artistry born in a world of tools.

When the clay slips and takes a dive,
Do I call for help or just high five?
Each flick and twist a giddy thrill,
Creating joy takes quite the skill!

But as it hardens, don't walk away,
For the pot might dance, or start to sway.
In the hands of creation, let it be,
A funny tale of pottery!

Serpentines of Longing

When pots collide in a playful way,
It's laughter's turn to save the day.
A twist, a turn, and oh what's that?
A serpent in the midst, imagine that!

With wiggly lines, their shadows trace,
A dance of clay, a quirky embrace.
Will it hold the giggles or just a fish?
I'd rather it dance than fulfill my wish!

Though it seems absurd, I give a wink,
A playful pot that needs a drink.
Could a clay cup have a craving so,
To twirl and whirl, oh where will it go?

Serpentines swirl where dreams take flight,
A comedic spin, oh what a sight!
Between the curves, there's mischief found,
In a world of clay, we're joyfully bound!

Soft Curves and Gentle Hands

With hands like clouds, I shape the clay,
Soft curves emerging in a playful fray.
Gentle nudges here, and a giggle there,
What will emerge—perhaps a bear?

Does this rough lump hold a pot so fine?
Or is it just a prank in design?
Laughter brewing as the wheel spins round,
In a world of pottery, joy is found!

With gentle hands, I paint a smile,
Creating magic with every style.
A bowl for soup, or a hat for fun,
Who knew clay could bring such a run?

So here we mix, we mold and play,
Soft curves whisper secrets of the day.
In clay we trust, with hands so grand,
Making memories, it's all quite planned!

Glazed Hopes

In the glaze, my hopes do shine,
A rainbow's touch, a glass of wine.
Will it crack under pressure or hold the toast?
I'm just here for the laughs, let's raise a roast!

With every layer, a story blooms,
A quirky pot for silly rooms.
Oh look, it's now the color of peas,
Hosting a party for all my keys!

High-fired humor and berry stains,
It's not a vessel; it's a wit that reigns.
Will it serve the pie or just steal the scene?
Creating pots like a patchwork dream!

In glazed hopes, we trust and play,
Cups that cheer and pots that sway.
So find your joy in bumps and grins,
In the art of clay, the fun begins!

Patterns of Connection

In a garden, pots align,
With secrets that intertwine.
Cracks that whisper, jokes that play,
Who knew plants had so much to say?

A daisy flirts with a shy fern,
In a pot, love takes a turn.
The soil giggles, roots in a twist,
Oh, what fun they can't resist!

Drips of water drop like tears,
On clay faces, laughter steers.
Who needs diamonds, gold, or pearls?
When pot plants are the coolest girls!

Together they share a quirky dance,
With every breeze, a little chance.
No need for fancy, high-cultured lore,
Just stay potted, forever more!

Silhouettes of Sentiment

Shadows stretch at dusk's warm gleam,
Two pots sit, a rooted dream.
With tea leaves brewing mischief near,
Laughter bubbles, it's all so clear.

One pot says, 'Oh, look at me!'
The other laughs, a sarcastic spree.
'You're just jealous of my plants,'
'But yours dance to all the wrong chants!'

A ladybug joins, a referee,
As pots argue, oh what glee!
Roots tussle like a playful brawl,
In their quarrels, love stands tall.

At night, under stars, they snicker,
The fairies add a little flicker.
Tiny twinkling in ceramic walls,
These pots are nuts! Well, that's their call!

Hearth Songs in Earthenware

In the kitchen, pots align,
As wooden spoons pour out the wine.
A basil leaf winks, sassy and bold,
This kitchen's a show, to be retold!

Oven warms with a chuckle loud,
While pots brag about their cloud.
They simmer and bubble, a melody,
Stirring up a tasty symphony!

Sassy thyme and pepper chat,
As two clay pots share a spat.
'You're too salty,' one does tease,
'At least I'm not as bland as peas!'

With each gust from the oven's heat,
They sing their songs, oh what a feat!
Cooking up laughter, meals divine,
In this pantry land where hearts entwine!

Heartfelt Imprints

On a shelf, clay friends reside,
Worn and chipped, but full of pride.
They tell tales of spills and stains,
Of clumsy hands and silly gains.

A cactus jokes 'I'm prickly tough!'
While other pots say, 'That's just rough!'
Their laughter echoes, fills the air,
A family bond beyond compare.

The herbs groove to a jolly beat,
As sunlight dances with their feet.
'With a little water, I'll bloom in time!'
'You mean with a little rhyme, oh what a crime!'

In this quirky house, where clay pots play,
Each bump and crack tells a fun display.
They cherish the moments, thick and thin,
For in every clay, there's joy within!

Reflections of You

In a garden of giggles and silly chats,
Your smile blooms like daisies, how about that?
With pots of fortune, we plant our dreams,
Mixing laughter and mischief in all our schemes.

Every glance, a tickle, every wink, a tease,
You steal my cookies, that's just not fair!
Yet here we are, with clumsy hearts,
Trying to dance, in this whirlwind of flair.

Cradled Desires

Underneath the moonlight, we share our pies,
You trip on the lawn; oh, how I'll cry!
Our wishes wrapped in chocolate and cream,
With marshmallow dreams and whipped-up steam.

Your spoon's in my yogurt, it's quite a sight,
We giggle and fumble, but everything's right.
In this playful mess, our secrets unfold,
In sweet silly laughter, we find love bold.

Unearthed Passions

Digging through dirt, my heart fizzes and sparks,
We plant our footprints, leaving silly marks.
In pots of delight, we bury our fears,
Watered with chuckles and maybe a few tears.

You juggle the onions, I toss in some spice,
Cooking our futures, oh, isn't it nice?
With mishaps we blossom, no holds barred,
Creating a garden that's truly bizarre.

Fire and Earth Unite

Combining our chaos like fire and clay,
Your dance of the flames makes me sway.
With giggles erupting, and spills we'll embrace,
Together, we'll conquer, this frantic race.

In the heat of the moment, we playfully tease,
While shaping our pot into whatever it sees.
With laughter as fuel, we'll craft and ignite,
Two silly hearts, dancing through the night.

Heartbeats Cast in Kiln Light

In a pot made of clay, we both sit tight,
Laughter in glazes, adding pure delight.
Mismatched handles, yet somehow they fit,
Firing through giggles, we can't help but split.

Chips on the rim, oh what a cute flaw,
Each little crack just adds to the awe.
Together we spin on this wheel of a day,
A sculpture of moments, all vibrant and gay.

With each turn of the clay, our stories unfold,
A masterpiece baked, with each touch we mold.
Painted with laughter, and a sprinkle of glee,
In the kiln of our hearts, you're my favorite spree.

So here's to our art, in this quirky embrace,
With every odd curve, there's a smile on your face.
Let's shape the mundane, make it wildly unique,
In our joyous creation, there's no room for bleak.

Cherished Shapes of Togetherness

In a studio filled with laughter and cheer,
We mold our adventures, year after year.
I drop a few blobs, you just roll your eyes,
But it's hard to stay mad when I'm caught in your sighs.

Our cups don't match, it's a charming collection,
Sipping our tea, we're an odd intersection.
Handles mismatched, oh what a delight,
Crack a wide smile, let's bask in the night.

Making small pots, with no real intent,
Yet filling them up with joy, heaven-sent.
Each little mishap, a story to keep,
As we laugh through the night, then fall fast asleep.

Our hearts are the clay, pliable and free,
Shaping a future that's all about glee.
In this workshop of whimsy, let's dance and play,
Cherished creations, come what may.

Each Turn a Memory

At the wheel we spin, our hands go round,
Each time you smile, the happiness found.
Throwing our worries, they just slip away,
  Creating pure joy on this goofy clay day.

With each funny fumble, we nurture the mess,
  Laughter erupts, oh, we're truly blessed.
A pot here, a bowl there, why not a vase?
Our clay-crafted dreams are a silly embrace.

Every quick turn is a moment so sweet,
  In our pottery studio, chaos is neat.
With slip on your nose, you're a sight to behold,
  Each turn a new memory, a story retold.

We fire up our hearts, just like in the kiln,
With humor and warmth, all the cool kids chill.
Embracing each fluke, with laughter we're rich,
In the art of creation, we've found our true niche.

Elements of Affection in Earthenware

In the clanking of tools, we find our sweet rhyme,
Crafting our dreams, one mess at a time.
Each little drip, oh what a fine sight,
We giggle so hard that it feels just right.

With fingers all muddy, we shape and we sway,
In this kiln of affection, where giggles hold sway.
You laugh as I drop, I laugh when you squish,
These simple moments, our clay-sculpted wish.

In earthen delights, we find our true cheer,
Creating each piece, year after year.
Like pots with their stains, we embrace every flaw,
In our playful adventure, there's magic in the raw.

So here's to the crafts, in our quirky abode,
Where laughter's the glue, and joy is the code.
We sculpt the mundane, with joy we declare,
In this world made of clay, nothing can compare.

Emotions Shaped by Hand

I crafted my feelings, oh what a mess,
A heart made of clay, it's anyone's guess.
I shaped it with giggles, a pinch of delight,
But it wobbled and wiggled, oh what a sight!

With each little poke, it grew quite a shape,
Rounder than dough, all slippery drape.
It fell off the wheel, rolled under the bench,
Now it sits in the corner, not quite the stench!

A heart needs some care, or so they all say,
But mine just prefers to bounce and to play.
Mold it, don't fold it, make sure that it's fun,
For shapes made with laughter, outshine all the sun!

I'll fix it with humor, a touch of pure glee,
Crafting my feelings, how hard can it be?
Emotions are clay, but not quite the norm,
In this goofy old studio, I weather the storm!

The Pottery of Your Smile

Your grin is a vessel, a bowl full of cheer,
It sparkles like sunshine, come on, let's hear!
With curves that enchant and a glaze so divine,
I'd trade all my mugs just to say you're all mine.

Your laughter's a rhythm, a potter's own tune,
It spins like the wheel 'neath the glow of the moon.
Each chuckle a brushstroke, each teardrop a glaze,
Creating a masterpiece that brightens my days.

Let's sculpt some new moments, just you and me,
With donuts for handles and jelly for glee.
We'll toss all the troubles into a big kiln,
And fire them away with a skip and a spin!

Your smile is a treasure, a quirky old find,
It's shaped like a heart, yet oozes refined.
So let's bake up some joy, just ready to serve,
This pottery laughter, it swerves and it curves!

Soft Glaze of Sweet Devotion

With each little brush, I paint on the love,
In shades of deep giggles and skies up above.
It's layered in whimsy, with sparkle and shine,
A canvas of joy, oh how playful divine!

Your quirks are the colors, a palette so bright,
Each chuckle a hue, like day turns to night.
We'll throw all our worries into the soft clay,
And mold up a romance that's silly and gay.

This bowl of affection, it's squishy yet firm,
With edges that wobble, it bends but won't squirm.
We'll serve up hilarity, a feast for our souls,
A dessert of pure whimsy that never grows old.

Each glaze tells a story, each crack is a tale,
Of laughter we shared in the warmth of the sail.
So let's spin our desires, our funky old dance,
In a workshop of giggles, true love's just by chance!

Hearths Fired with Longing

In the kiln of desire, we stoke up the flame,
With laughter so loud, it's hard to explain.
The logs of our dreams crackle under the glee,
As sparks of affection begin to run free.

We toss in some wishes, a sprinkle of fun,
A whiff of your smile, boy, isn't that one?
The heat of our hearts, oh how bright it can glow,
As we dance around fires, it's all for the show!

We shape every moment, like clay in our grip,
With snickers and secrets, let's take a quick sip.
We'll forge our connections with playful delight,
In the hearth of our longing, we'll giggle all night.

So here's to the warmth of this quirky abode,
Where laughter's the currency and joy's the code.
In this oven of cheer where we both live and play,
We'll craft pieces of wonder, come join in, hooray!

Dust and Dreams

In a little pot, some dust collects,
What a fine place for our little specs!
With dreams so tall, they wobble a bit,
Let's see if they'll sprout or just sit.

I sprinkled my heart with a touch of cheer,
Add a dash of giggles, oh dear, oh dear!
With every crack, a laugh should bloom,
Maybe next week, they'll make a room.

Oh, lost in thoughts of what might grow,
A tiny flower? Or just a show?
The clay's so playful, it curls and rolls,
Who knew dry dust could have such goals?

For every tumble, let's raise a toast,
To dreams that flounder, we love them most!
So here's to us and our earthly stake,
Creating chaos from simple clay!

Together We Shape

With hands so muddy, we craft away,
Making odd forms that brighten the day.
Together we giggle, oh what a sight,
Is that a vase or a hidden delight?

Our laughter echoes as we twist and turn,
Creating strange shapes for the world to learn.
A playful jug or a silly bowl,
Every creation speaks to the soul.

We mold with vigor, the fun won't cease,
Striving for beauty, yet finding our peace.
In every mishap, there's a bit of grace,
A masterpiece born from a silly face.

So let's keep shaping this art of ours,
With bumps and giggles, we reach the stars.
In every curve, our joy shines bright,
Together we shape, it feels just right!

Interwoven with Clay

In a spinny wheel, we dance and play,
Life's tangled knots, we smooth away.
With every pinch, our silliness flows,
Creating some wonders, who really knows?

A bowl shaped like a perplexed cat,
Or perhaps a mug, just look at that!
With laughter bubbling, we spin and cheer,
Each piece we mold brings a little near.

The clay, it slips through our fingertips fast,
But we're making memories that are sure to last.
Each swirl and twist tells a tale of glee,
Even if it ends as a wobbly spree!

For art is found in the funny and wack,
Embracing the crooked, we'll never look back.
Interwoven, we laugh, it's more than a game,
In this priceless mess, we'll make our name!

The Fragility of Form

A pot so fine, but oh so weak,
It holds our secrets, but can't even speak.
With every hug, it starts to shake,
This fragile piece, what will it take?

I served a soup in a crooked bowl,
One sip, and laughter was the goal.
With every spill, we'd toast and frown,
Who knew clay could wear such a crown?

The cracks, they whisper of stories near,
Each flaw a token, let's hold it dear.
A fragile thing, yet full of glee,
With silly dances, just you and me!

So raise your mugs, let's drink this cheer,
In every wobble, we find our sphere.
For form might be fragile, but oh so fun,
Together we play, two hearts as one!

In the Shadows of Our Creation

In the workshop, we both trip,
Clumsy hands, a funny slip.
Your smile's a glaze I want to keep,
As pots and giggles make us leap.

We mold the clay, we toss the bowl,
Contorted shapes, we lose control.
A lopsided heart, just like my hair,
We laugh, create without a care.

Your silly face, it cracks me up,
Oh, how we twist the future cup.
A vase that holds our raucous cheer,
With every clay-smudged, charming sneer.

Together, we'll spin this merry wheel,
A sticky mess, but oh, the feel.
Our clunky art, quite the display,
In every flaw, our hearts will play.

When Hearts Learn to Fire

In the kiln, our hearts ignite,
Burning bright in pure delight.
A dance of flames, a playful glow,
Like marshmallows toasted, oh what a show!

Your laughter crackles in the heat,
As clay and giggles find their beat.
We shape the dreams with frolic and fun,
In a pot that holds two, oh so undone.

The fire pops, and so do we,
Hilarity wrapped in pottery.
A friendship fierce, like a wicked spark,
Each silly moment, leaving a mark.

With every crack, we just can't stop,
Our sculpted joy, on top of the flop.
Together we forge, with smiles so bright,
In this crazy kiln, everything feels right.

Fragile Heart

Oh, don't you dare give me those eyes,
So delicate, they've got me in ties.
A fragile love, like pottery thin,
I'll keep it safe, but where do I begin?

A gentle tap, and there it goes,
Your whimsical laugh, heaven knows.
We craft our dreams as if they're glass,
With every giggle, we let time pass.

It's tricky, this dance of care,
With clumsy fingers, I barely dare.
But when you smile, all risks are tossed,
In our little world, nothing's lost.

So I'll glue the pieces when they break,
And laugh it off for our fun's sake.
For in this fragile, silly art,
We find the strength to mend the heart.

Sturdy Vessel

A vessel built from goofy schemes,
In this clay game, we're wild with dreams.
You've made a cup that's strong and bold,
While I just giggle, my hands controlled.

The jokes are thick, like our clay mix,
Your puns stick better than any tricks.
With every twist, we share a laugh,
In our sturdy pot, we find our path.

So let's build something that won't break,
With every touch, let's create our stake.
This rough-hewn vessel, oh what a sight,
Holding all our silliness, shining bright.

In laughter's grip, together we'll stand,
A sturdy bond, hand in hand.
Through every wobble, we'll find our way,
In this funny world, we choose to stay.

Sculpted Emotions

With every squeeze, my heart can mold,
A laughter story that never gets old.
You shape the joy with a quirky grin,
In our clay adventure, let the fun begin!

We push and pull, just like the clay,
Turning dull moments into play.
Your goofy faces, all so bright,
In this art class, we own the night.

With every stroke, our quirkiness shows,
As we mold our dreams in jiggly flows.
Oh, watch out now for the flurry of laughs,
In this sculpted world, we're both the crafts!

So here we stand, our art's the proof,
Creating memories, always aloof.
In this mishmash of clay and cheer,
Our hearts find joy as we persevere.

Echoes Within the Vessel

In a pot so round and tight,
Two hearts quip in pure delight.
Their laughter spills, not a drop missed,
Like spills from a pot rushed by a twist.

They dance on the rim, oh what a sight!
Chasing dreams in the dim twilight.
Their jokes like clay, molded with cheer,
Even the flowers lean in to hear!

Careful now, don't tip too fast,
Or the giggles will surely outlast.
A crack or two? Just character, see!
In this silly tale of you and me.

So here they swirl, in a twirling play,
Their silly secrets, a potter's clay.
With every joke, their hearts they mold,
Echoes of laughter, forever bold.

Seasoned by Time

Stirring flavors in a quirky space,
Where spices mingle, a happy place.
They sprinkle joy like seasoned salt,
In this kitchen, smiles never halt.

Amidst the pots, their stories simmer,
Each tale a giggle, each tear a shimmer.
They've pan-fried worries, sautéed regret,
Cooking up laughter, their finest duet.

Oh, look at them, dance with flair,
Whisking up chaos, but they don't care.
Time has poured out its vintage wine,
Yet they sip joy, always feeling fine.

Each meal a memory, seasoned delight,
In this banquet of love, everything's bright.
With every hearty laugh they share,
Time's gentle touch, in the pot's warm air.

Handcrafted Bonds

In a workshop filled with vibrant hue,
Two hands mold clay, just me and you.
With each push and pull, a bond so sweet,
Their giggles echo while they shape and meet.

Lumps of clay wear silly grins,
As they ponder where the fun begins.
With every turn, they spin a tale,
Of pots and pans, from small to pale.

They carved a heart, oh what a sight!
Mismatched pieces, yet fitting right.
A handle for hugs, and a base for laughs,
Each crack a memory, a quirky path.

In this mess of clay and sheer delight,
They find pure joy, shining so bright.
Handcrafted bonds, forever entwined,
With every chuckle, their hearts aligned.

Sculpture of Sincerity

A masterpiece formed from playful clay,
Where honesty blooms in a silly way.
No polish needed, just a goofy grin,
Their hearts sculpted with laughter within.

Each touch playful, each twist a treat,
Creating moments that can't be beat.
They chisel away at doubts and fears,
With every giggle, they find new gears.

With colors vibrant, they paint their dreams,
Adding whimsical flair, bursting at the seams.
A sculpture of joy, so bizarre yet true,
In this art of sincerity, it's just us two.

Through each funny shape, their spirits soar,
Every imperfection they can't ignore.
For in this clay, their love takes form,
A joyful creation, forever warm.

The Touch of a Sculptor

In a workshop bustling with clay,
Sculptor laughs, shaping hearts all day.
With a pinch and a twist, oh what fun,
Every piece tells a joke—everyone's won!

Molding lovers with a wink and a grin,
He adds a big nose, now let the fun begin!
These figures trot out with mismatched shoes,
A comedic dance, how could they lose?

When a vase starts to wobble, it's no great fear,
"Just pour in some giggles, and we'll cheer!"
For in this chaos, a smile takes flight,
Crafted by laughter, it feels so right.

At the end of the day, as they bask in the light,
These cheeky creations make the world bright.
With a wave and a laugh, they take a bow,
In the gallery of joy, they're the stars of now!

Embodied Whimsy

In a field of laughter where the wild things bloom,
Silly shapes arise, dispelling all gloom.
A bowl with a giggle, a plate with a snort,
Every piece tells a tale of playful rapport.

With hands made for mischief and eyes full of cheer,
Each sculpted piece holds laughter, my dear.
Two mugs dance together, a jig so absurd,
Making toast to the day with a clink and a word!

Among clanging clay, there's no time for frowns,
In this whimsical world, we're all wearing crowns.
Twisted together in a delightful embrace,
Each crackle and chip sings of love's silly grace.

So here's to creations that capture our hearts,
Crafted from humor, where the fun never departs.
In this merry garden, we'll all take a seat,
Sipping joy served with a whimsical beat.

Soulmates Shaped by Time

Two pots met by chance, in the sun's glowing light,
Spinning round on the wheel, it felt just right.
With a bit of a roll and a tumble here and there,
They crafted a bond, beyond compare.

One pot said, "I'll be the tall and the wise!"
The other replied, "I've got charm, just look in my eyes!"

Together they giggled, their edges entwined,
A duet of shapes, uniquely defined.

From the kiln of mishaps, they emerged together,
Potted buddies, in all kinds of weather.
With a hearty glaze, they shine ever so bright,
For even in flaws, they find delight.

At the end of the day, when the shelf's set just right,
These two silly pots twinkle in the night.
They're soulmates, you see, with quirks that delight,
Making the world giggle through every blight!

The Deepest Imprint

In the squishy heart of a studio dear,
Molded impressions bring laughter and cheer.
With every squeeze, a chuckle erupts,
These playful creations, oh how they disrupt!

A teapot with sass, a creamer with flair,
Each piece is a character, without a care.
When poured, they spill stories, with pumpkin spice glee,
In this clay-filled kingdom, it's all about glee!

Footprints of mishap tell tales as they go,
A giggle escapes when the pot starts to flow.
The fingerprints linger, like joy in a dream,
Celebrating chaos, the ultimate team!

So let's raise a glass to this whimsical song,
Where the imprints of laughter forever belong.
In this clay of delight, we find our own tune,
Crafted by giggles, our hearts in full bloom!

Earth's Warm Embrace

In the kitchen, pots start to dance,
Spaghetti noodles chasing romance.
With meatballs rolling like silly dreams,
Sauce splashes are more than it seems.

A spoon takes a twirl, it's quite the show,
Salt and pepper join, and off they go!
Pasta pirouettes, what a delight,
Cooking up chaos, a flavorful fight.

The Alchemy of Togetherness

Two awkward chefs in a tiny space,
Trying to cook with a smile on their face.
A pinch of chaos, a dash of fun,
Mixing up laughter 'til the day is done.

Spilling flour like it's confetti time,
Doughy hands clapping, a messy rhyme.
Stirring up giggles in every bowl,
Creating a feast that warms the soul.

Chiseled Expressions

Sculpting cakes with a playful spin,
Fondant faces that wear a grin.
Eyes made of candy, oh what a treat,
Every slice served with a dash of defeat.

Pies in the oven have started to sing,
Hot crusts with sass, oh what joy they bring!
Baking together, what a fun art,
Finding sweet moments in the tart.

Firing the Heart

In the kiln, the dishes twirl and spin,
Terracotta dreams, let the fun begin!
With potters' wheels making goofy tunes,
As clay squishes, they dance like loons.

Firing temperatures make things get wild,
A ceramic mug that's crazily compiled.
Quirky shapes, a love no one knew,
Crafted with laughter, and cheer, and skew.

Clay and Heartstrings Entwined

In the studio, we're a mess,
With splatters and molds, I must confess.
You threw a pot, I made a drip,
Yet in this chaos, our hearts still skip.

Laughter echoes, as clay takes flight,
Each squished attempt brings pure delight.
A wheel spins, and so do we,
Dancing on mud, in glee and spree.

We shape our dreams with silly grins,
Hmm, that vase looks like it has fins!
A pinch of joy, a laugh, a twist,
In our crafted world, nothing's amiss.

So grab your tools, let's make a mess,
Together we're art, nothing less.
In this funny dance of earth and fate,
Our hearts grow soft, oh isn't that great?

Sculpted Warmth of Togetherness

With every lump of clay we face,
Your cheeky grin brings sunny grace.
I'll mold a heart, you'll form a tree,
Together, we're quite the sight to see.

Your hands are dainty, my grip is bold,
Who knew pottery could make us gold?
A tilt, a twist, a comical fail,
Yet in our clumsiness, we prevail.

The kiln is hot, but so are we,
As we joke about what could be.
You're sculpting love, I'm making cups,
With every giggle, our spirit erupts.

In this warm studio, we find our way,
Turning mud into magic every day.
So here's to laughter and clay-smeared skin,
In this fun-filled mess, we both win!

Dreaming in Rustic Vases

Under the sun, we plot our fate,
Creating mishaps at a rapid rate.
You're making a jug, I'm forming a plate,
At this pottery wheel, we can't be late.

A rustic vase, but it looks like a blob,
You laugh so hard, I nearly sob.
Each quirky creation, a story to tell,
In our muddy world, we truly excel.

With hands so caked, we mold and spin,
What's that shape? Is it a cat or a fin?
We give it a name, a silly one so sweet,
In our tiny kingdom, we accept no defeat.

The clay may harden, but laughter stays,
In every blunder, our hearts amaze.
So let's keep dreaming, in this crazy space,
For joy's the true craft in our friendly race!

Heartfelt Echoes from the Kiln

The kiln is buzzing, can you hear?
Whispers of clay, laughter draws near.
You wrote my name on a teapot askew,
Yet it's a masterpiece, just like you.

In this crazy blend of heat and fun,
I threw a mug, you threw a pun.
With each tiny crack and every glaze,
We craft our bliss in the silliest ways.

Our pottery's star, it isn't precise,
But it glows with memories, and that's nice.
Fired with laughter, our art's alive,
In this playful chaos, together we thrive.

So let's embrace this quirky charm,
With clay and humor, we cause no harm.
In a world of vessels, we find our tune,
Echoing heartbeats beneath the moon.

www.ingramcontent.com/pod-product-compliance
Lightning Source LLC
Chambersburg PA
CBHW072213070526
44585CB00015B/1322